Christine Brady

Christine Brady

ART DECO
STAINED GLASS
PATTERN BOOK
91 Designs for Workable Projects

ART DECO
STAINED GLASS
PATTERN BOOK

91 Designs for Workable Projects

ED SIBBETT, JR.

DOVER PUBLICATIONS, INC.

New York

PUBLISHER'S NOTE

The geometrically oriented Art Deco style of the 1920s and 1930s is now permanently linked in the minds of most people with its applications in architecture, graphics, interior decoration and industrial design. But the two-dimensionality of most of the intricate geometric patterns, along with Art Deco's development of modern art's brilliant and unusual color schemes, also made this style perfect for the medium of stained glass. Many Art Deco designers rediscovered this craft and produced stunning works of amazing complexity and color.

This collection's 91 newly rendered, authentic Art Deco patterns are a rich source of ideas for stained glass workers and can be adapted for a variety of projects—windows, panels, lampshades, mirrors, mobiles and other crafts ideas. The designs are representative of a number of Art Deco trends: abstract patterns in both straight-line and curved motifs; stylized representations of men and women (in characteristic '20s garb); and the flowing forms of flowers and plants that seem to be a holdover from the Art Nouveau period at the turn of the century. Art Deco's sources and applications were many and varied, and the potential for experimentation and variety is still there for the modern stained glass worker.

Suppliers of glass and other materials, including general instruction books and tools for the beginner, should be listed in your local Yellow Pages.

Bibliographical Note

Art Deco Stained Glass Pattern Book is a new work, first published by Dover Publications, Inc., in 1977.

DOVER *Pictorial Archive* SERIES

International Standard Book Number

ISBN-13: 978-0-486-23550-9
ISBN-10: 0-486-23550-5

Manufactured in the United States by Courier Corporation
23550521
www.doverpublications.com

2

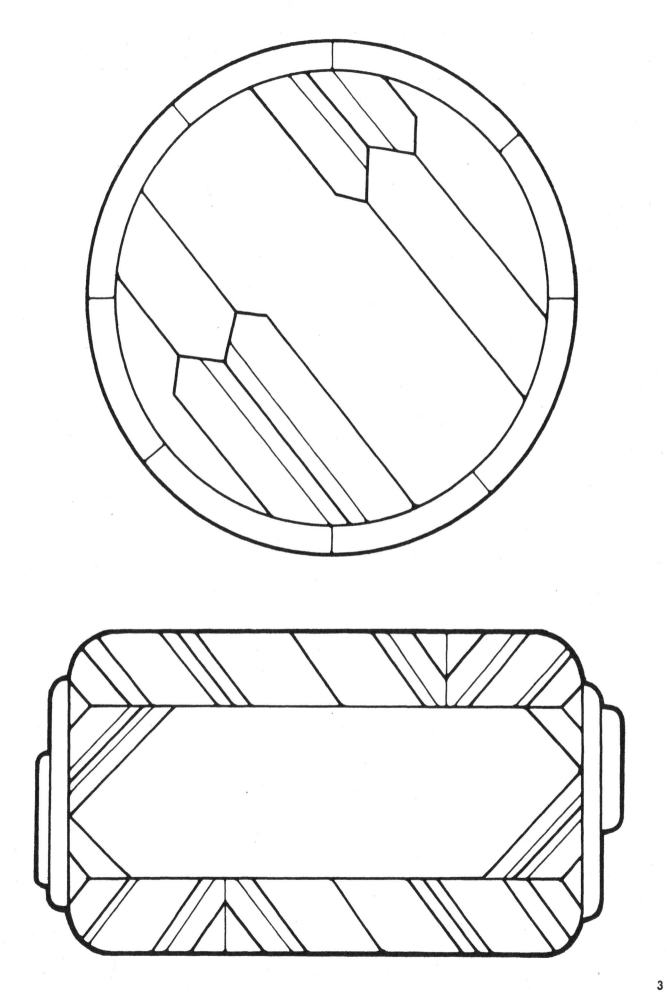

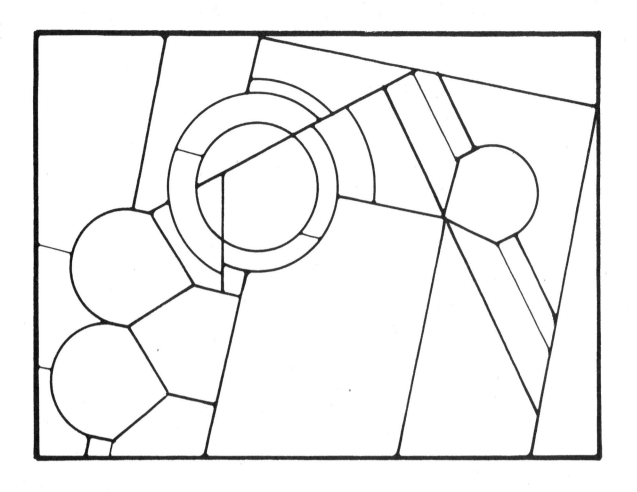

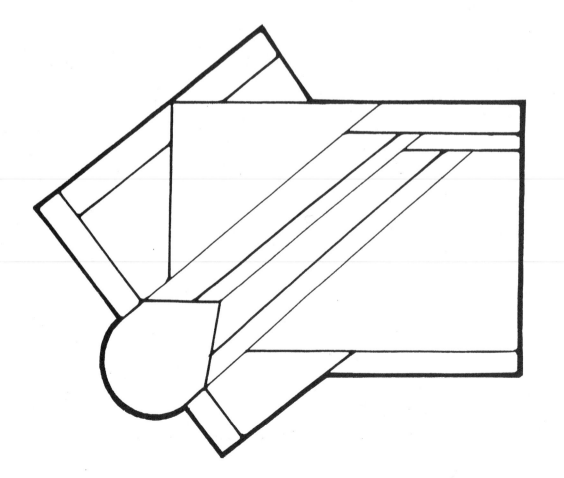

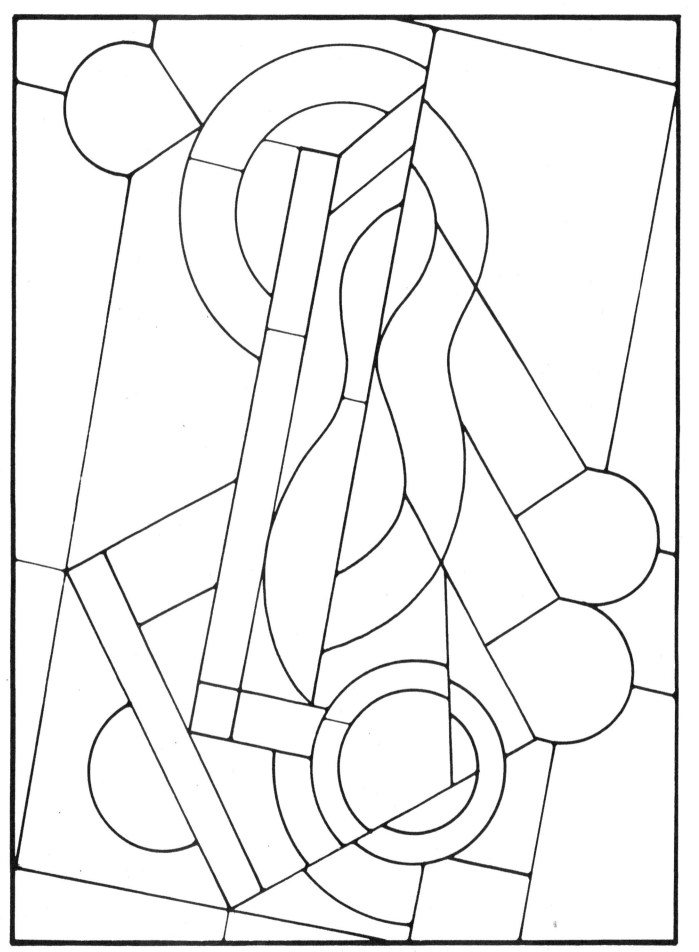

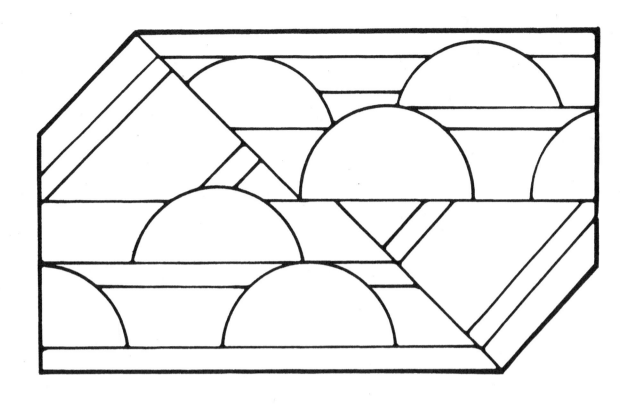

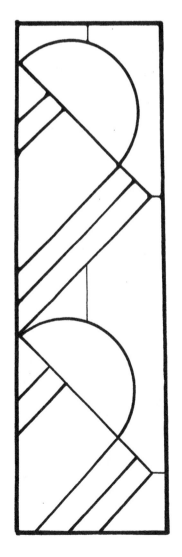

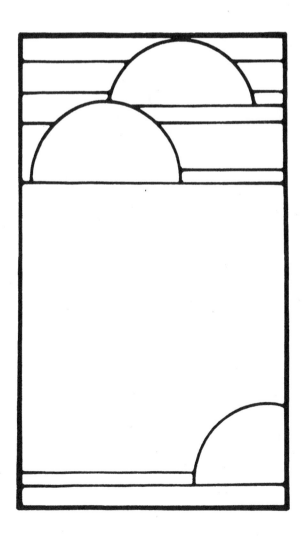

8

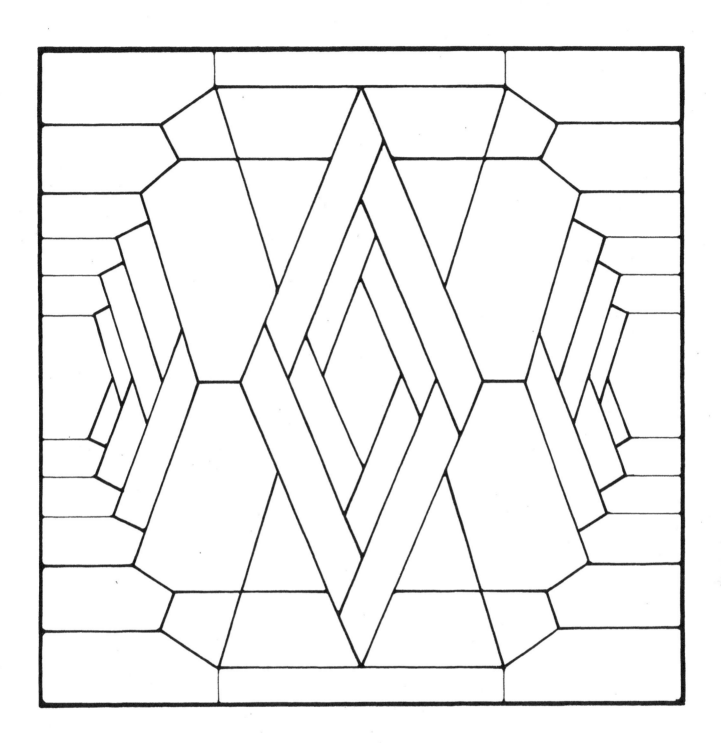

10

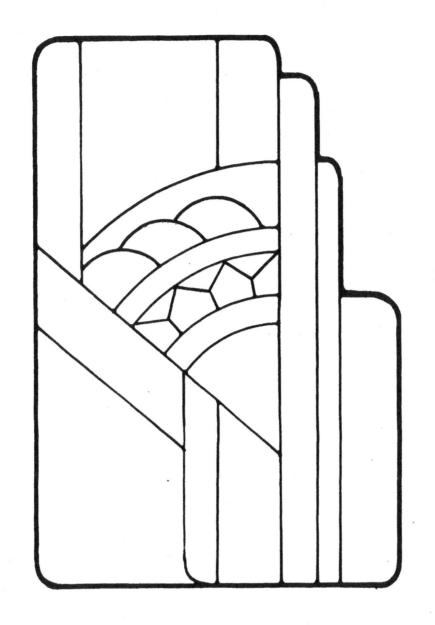

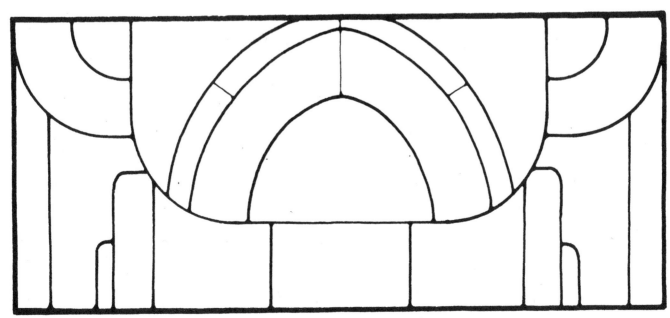

12

13

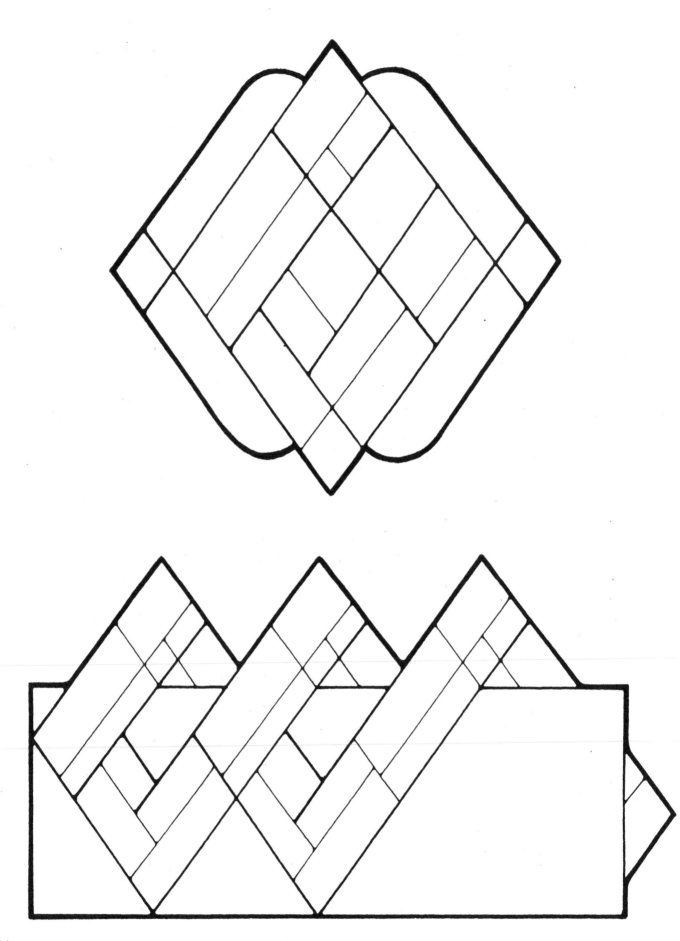

16

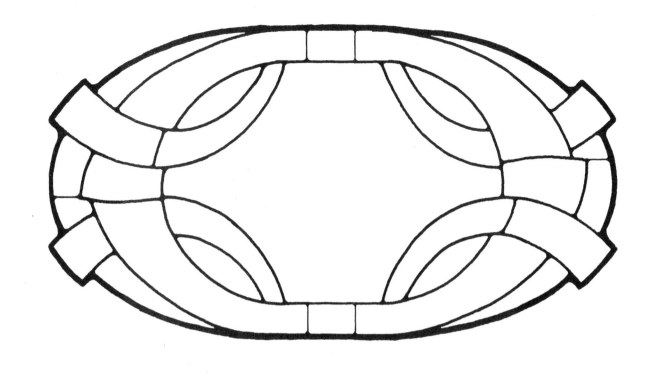

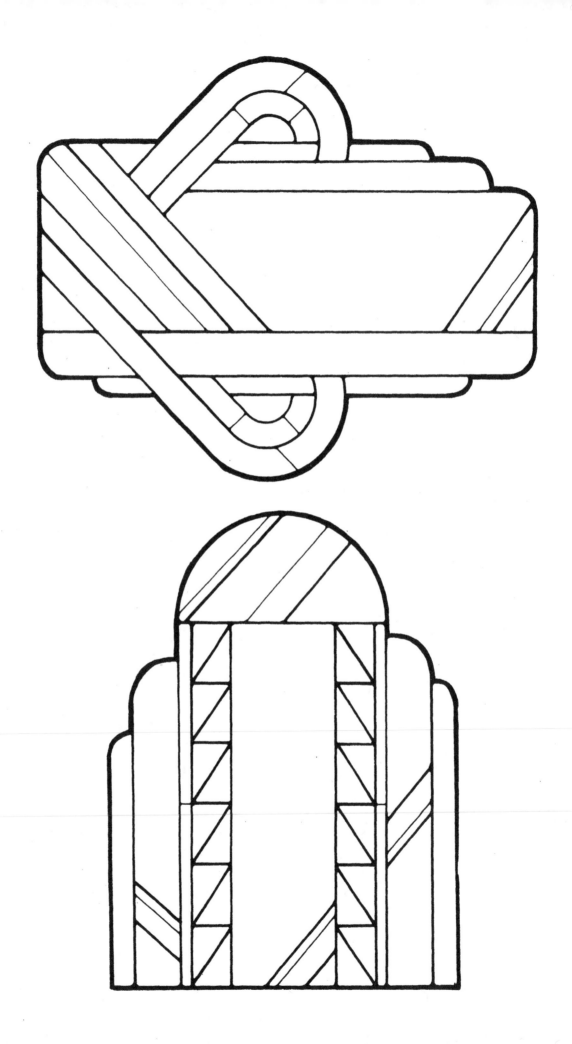

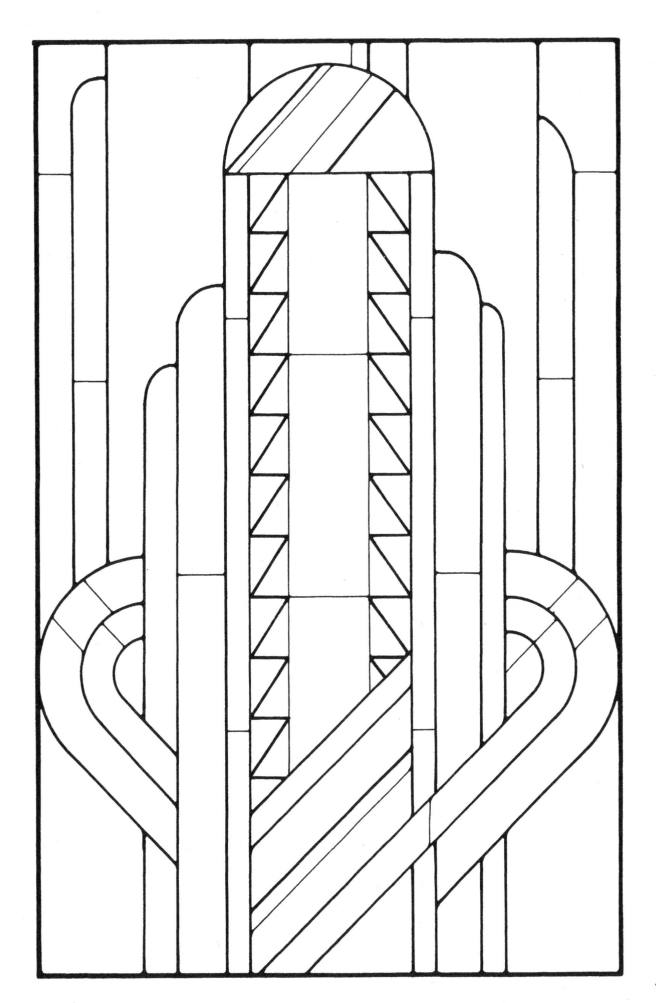

19

20

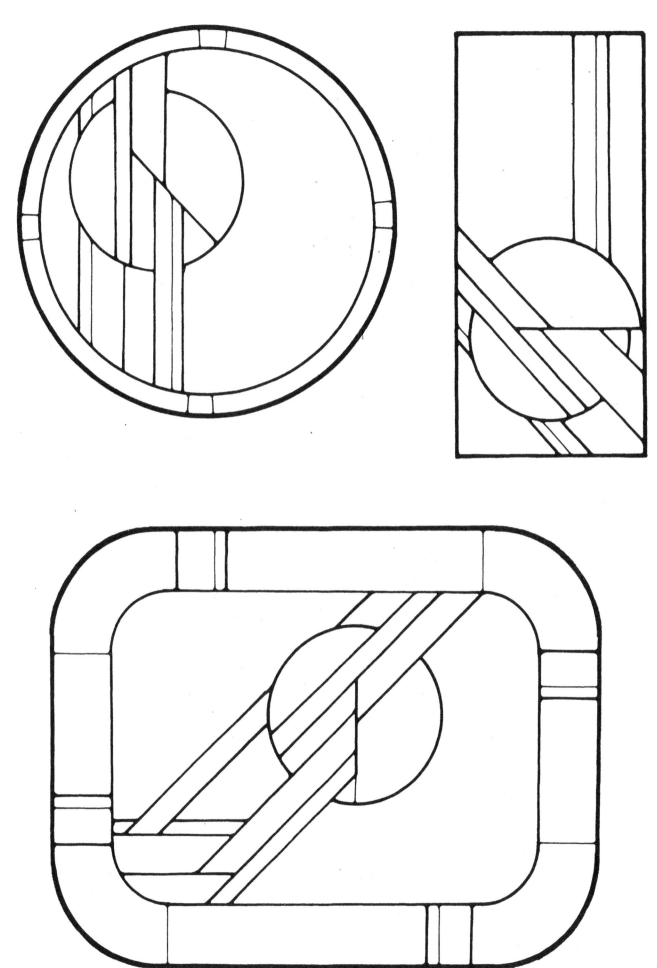

21

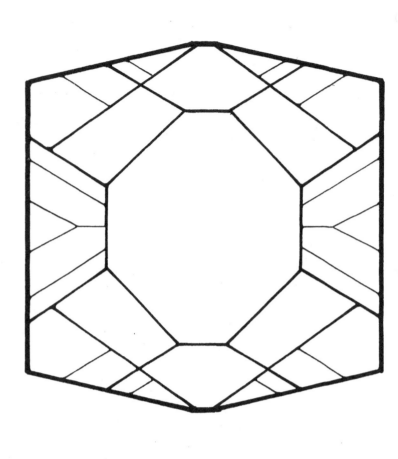

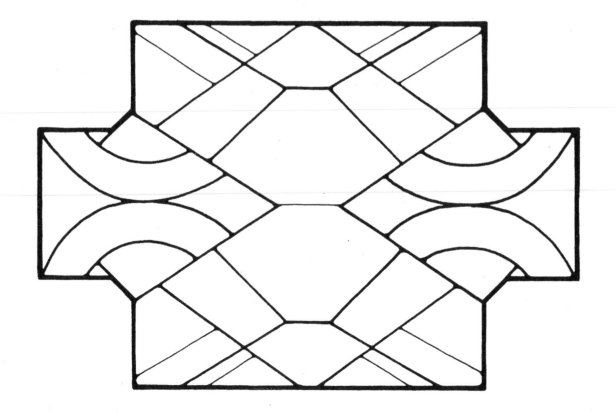

23

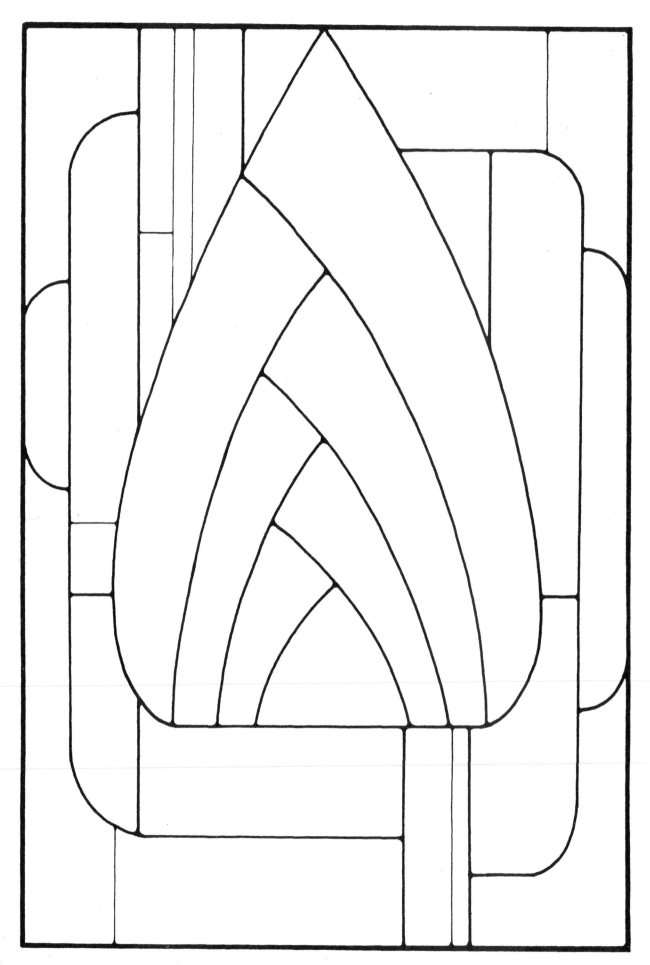

24

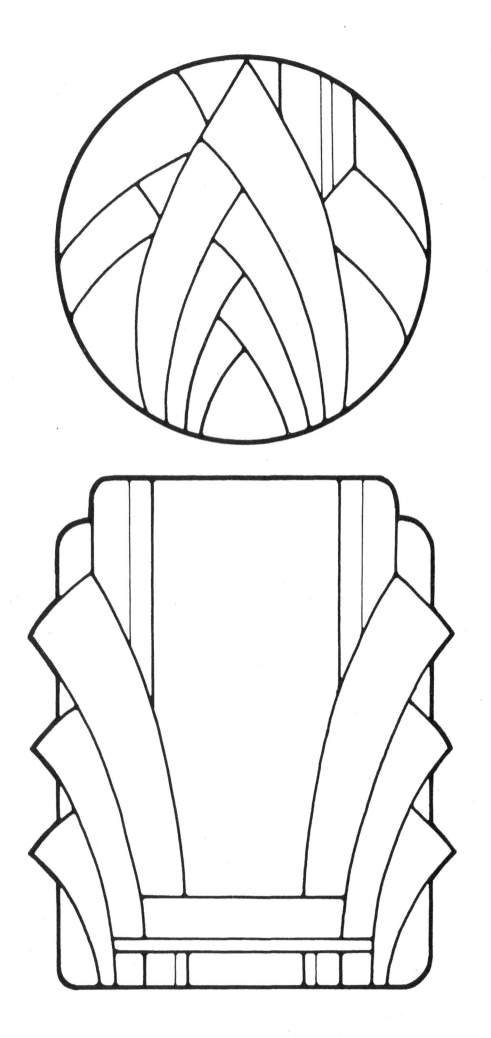

25

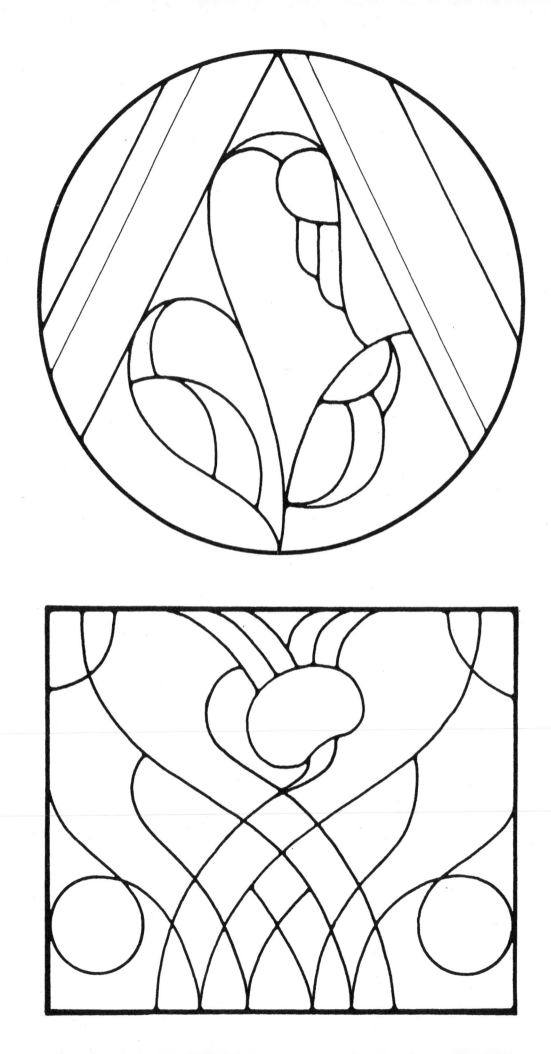

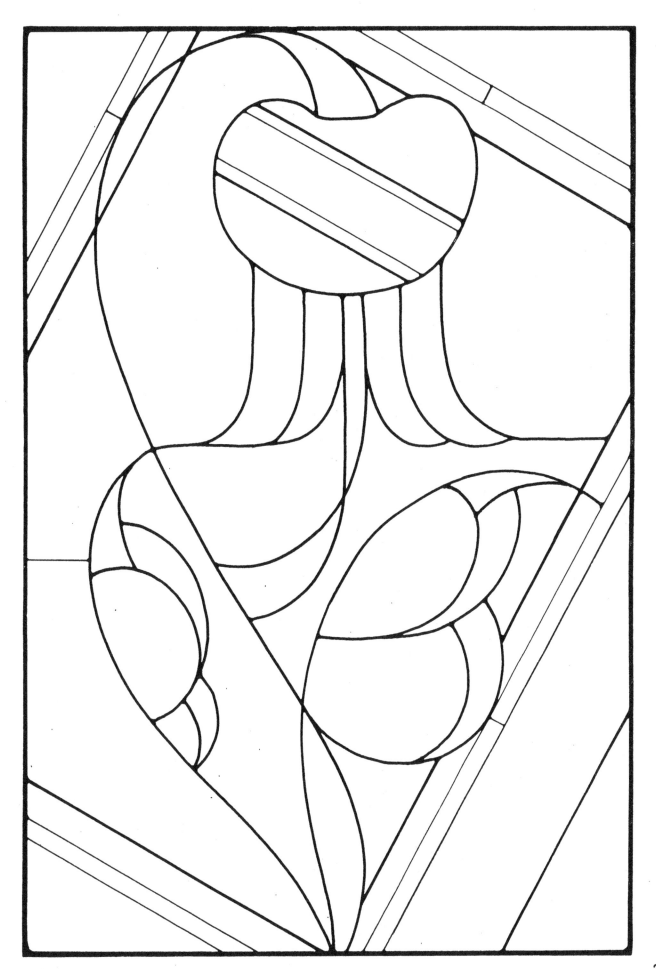

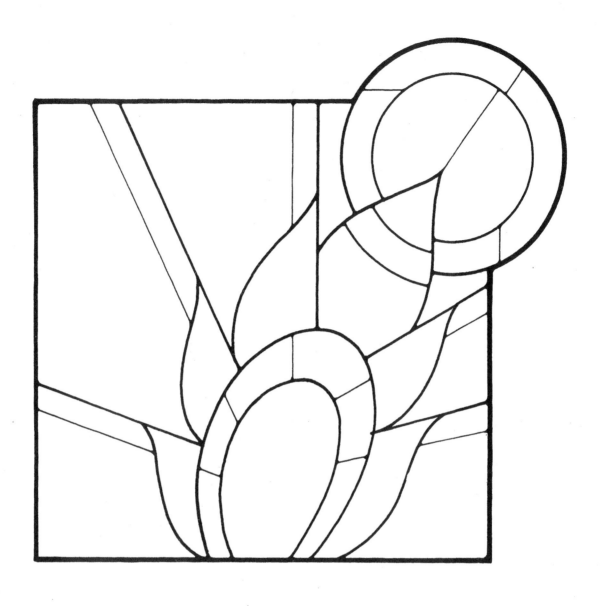

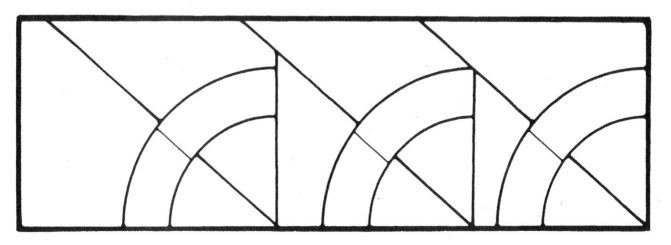

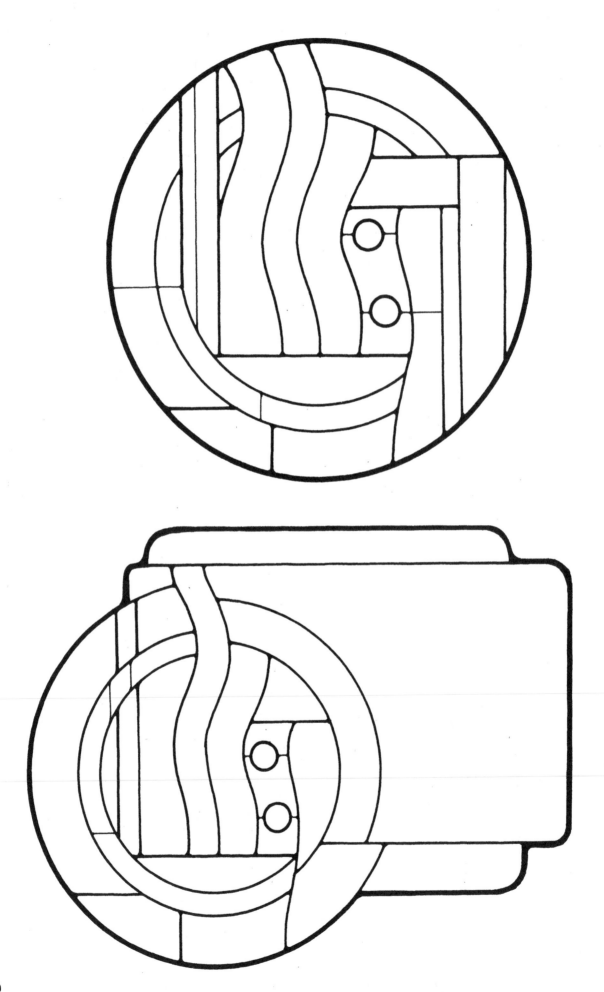

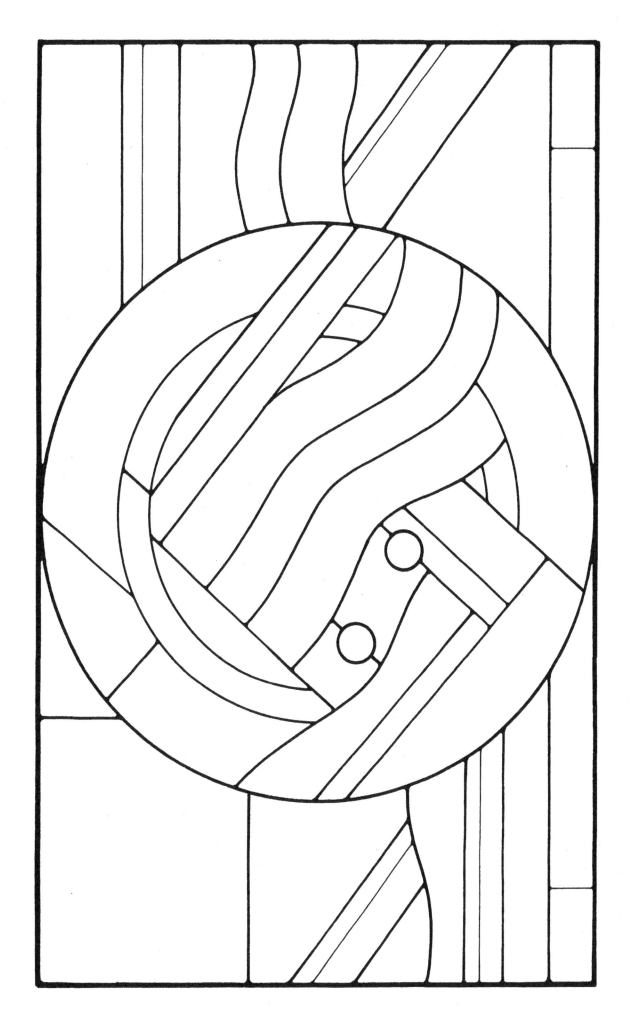

31

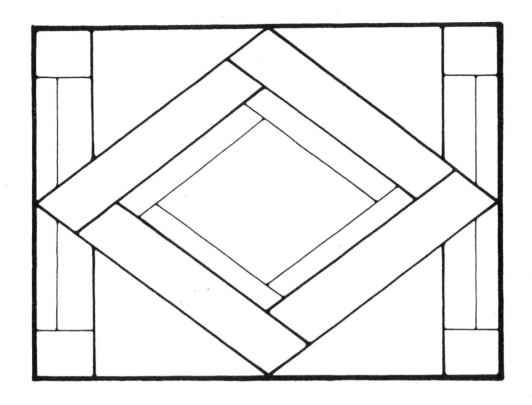

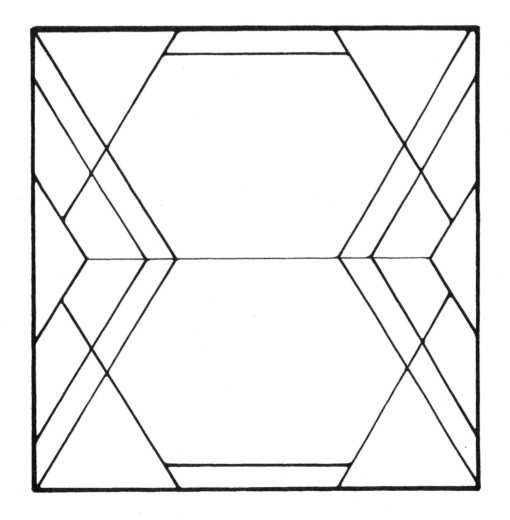

33

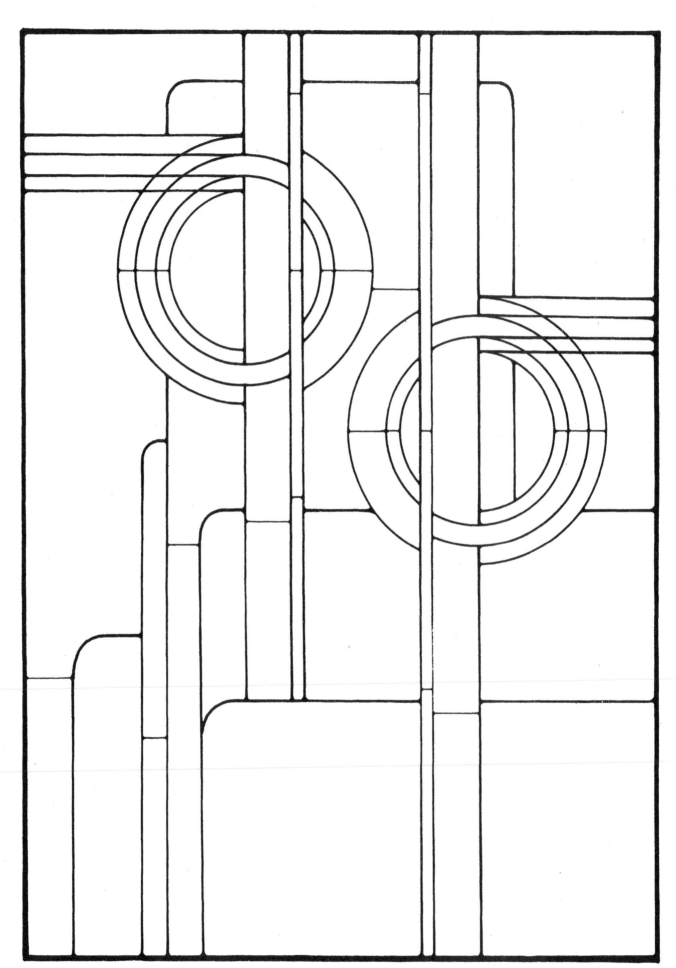

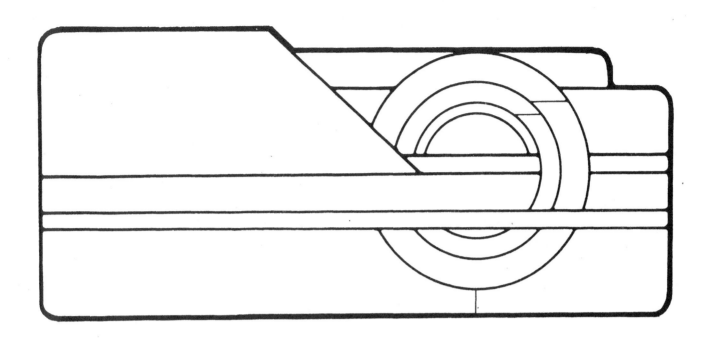

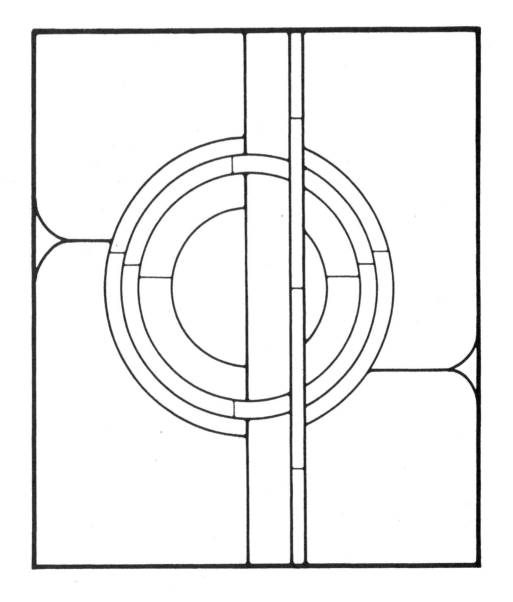

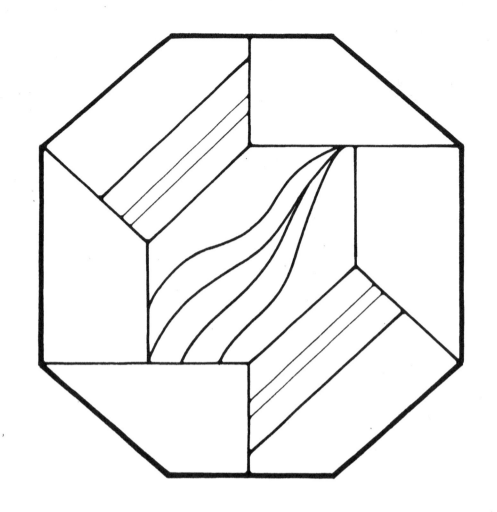

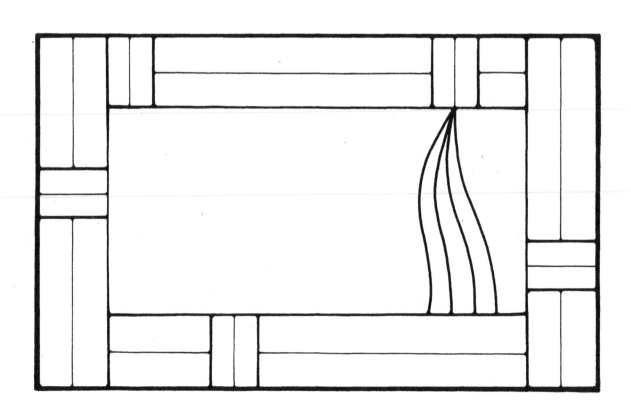

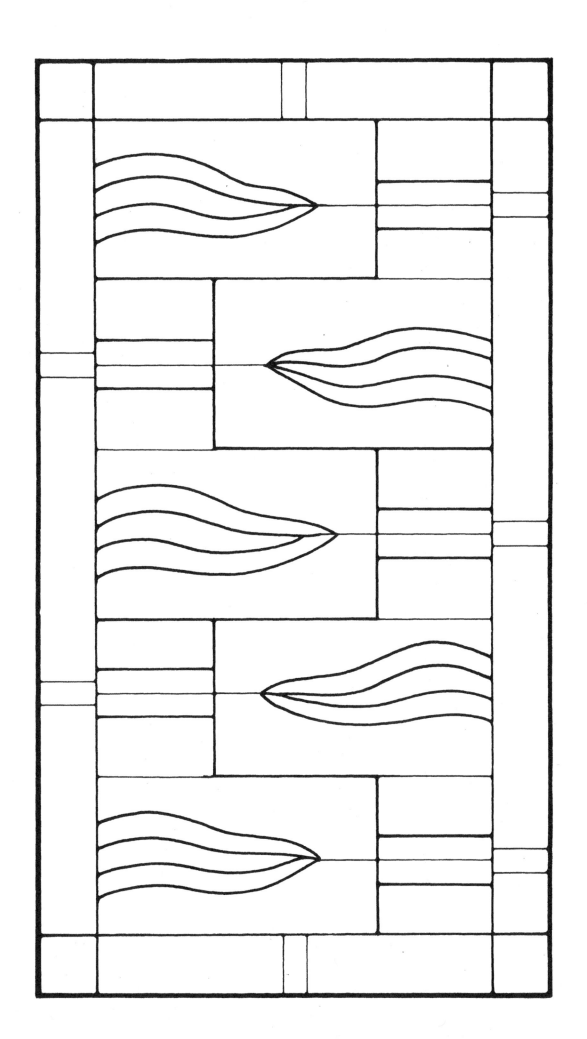

40

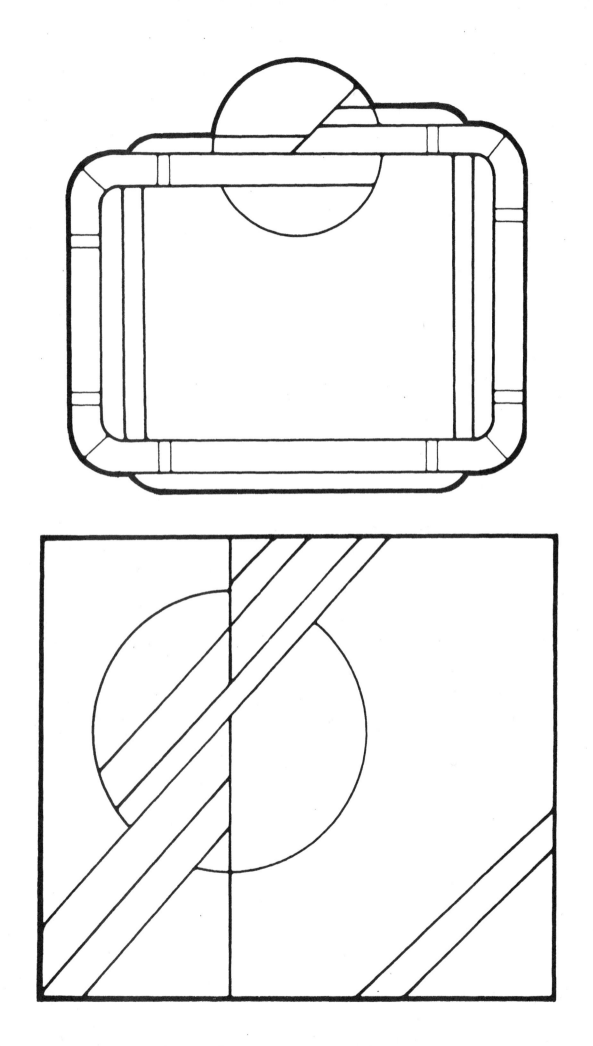

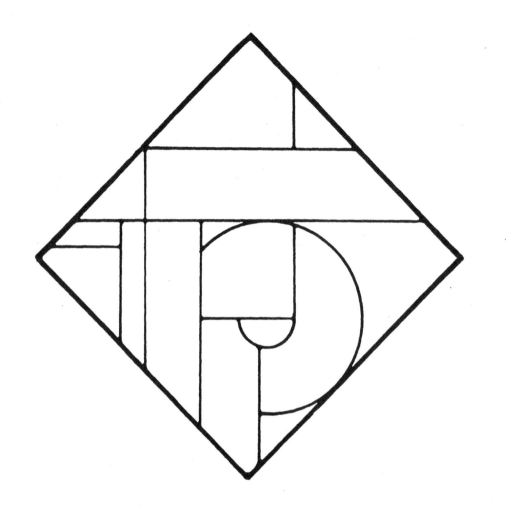

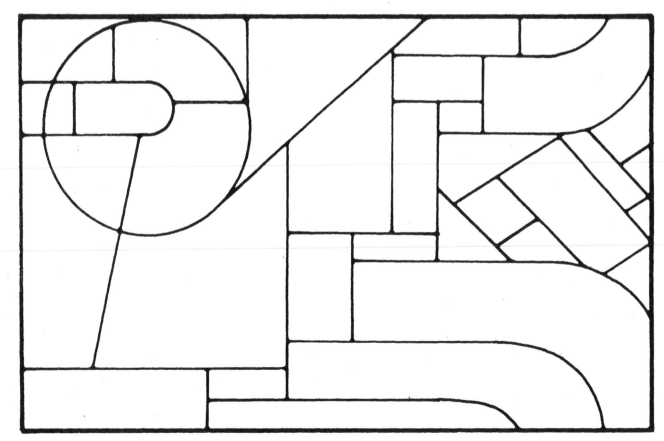

44

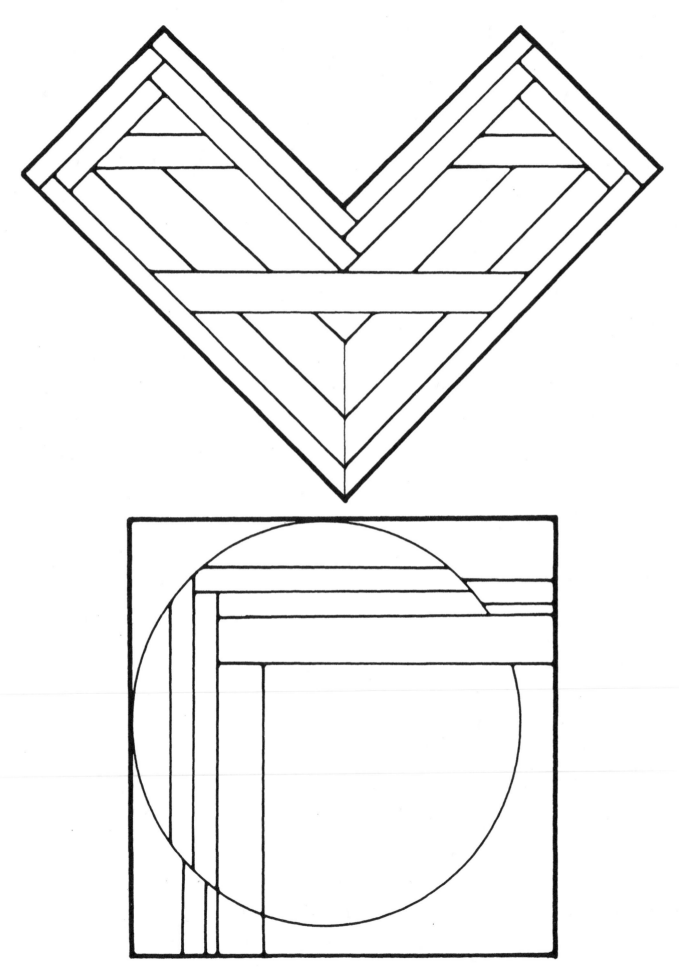

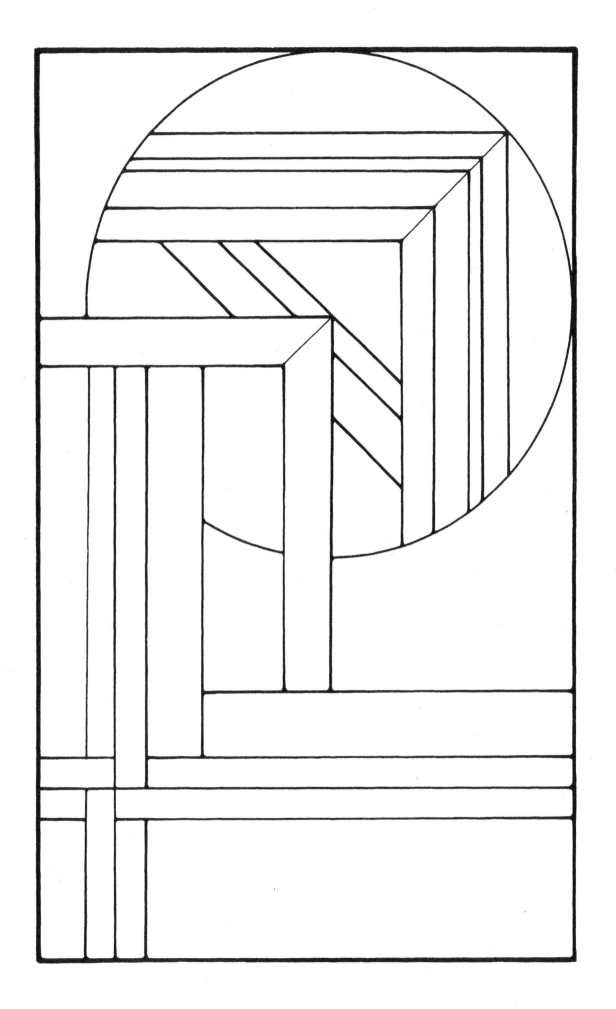

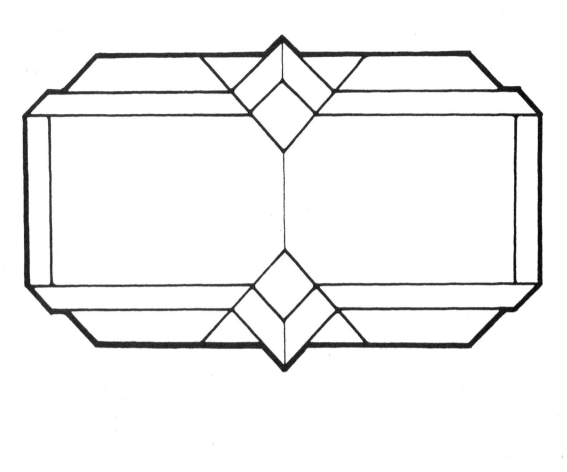

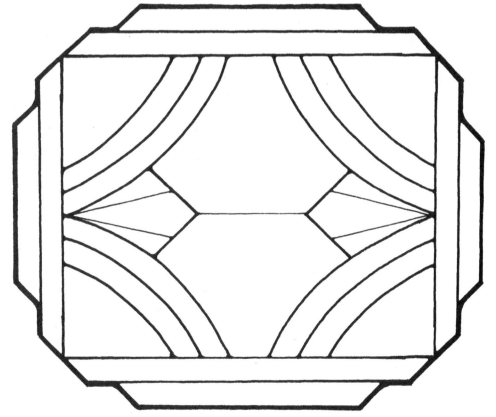

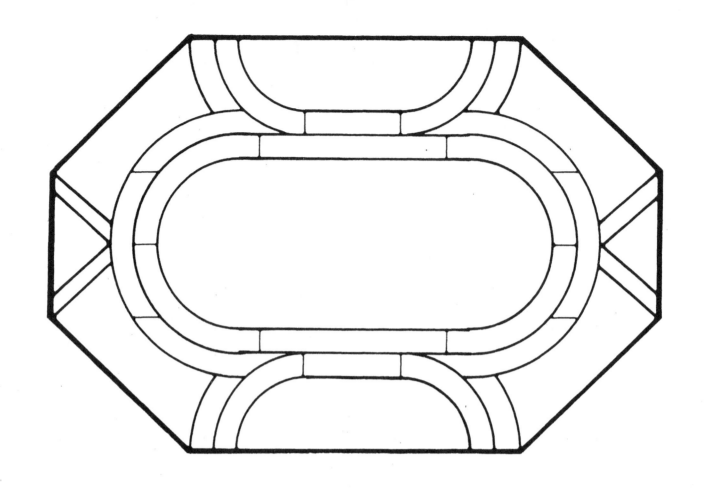

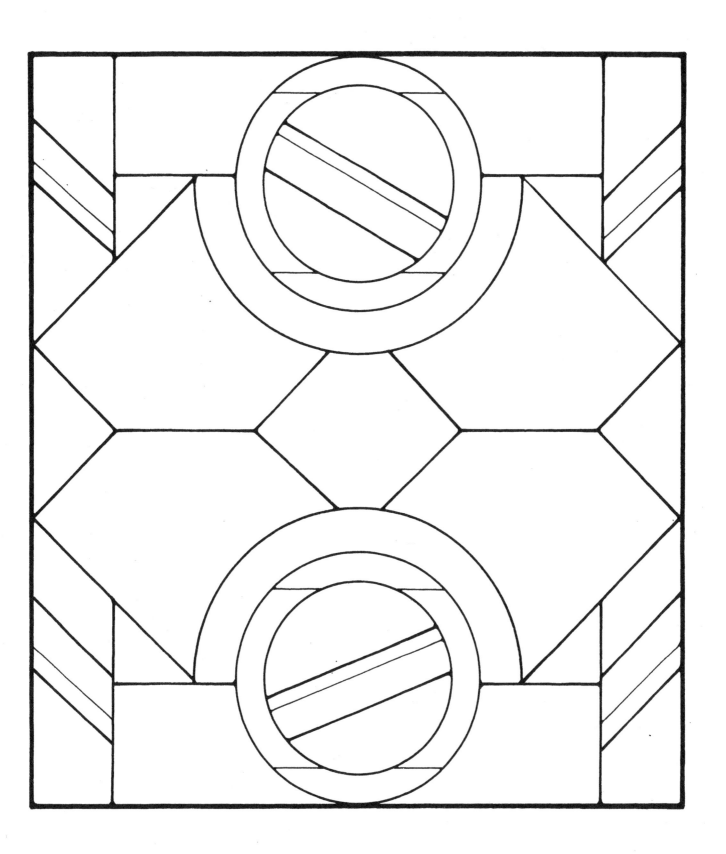

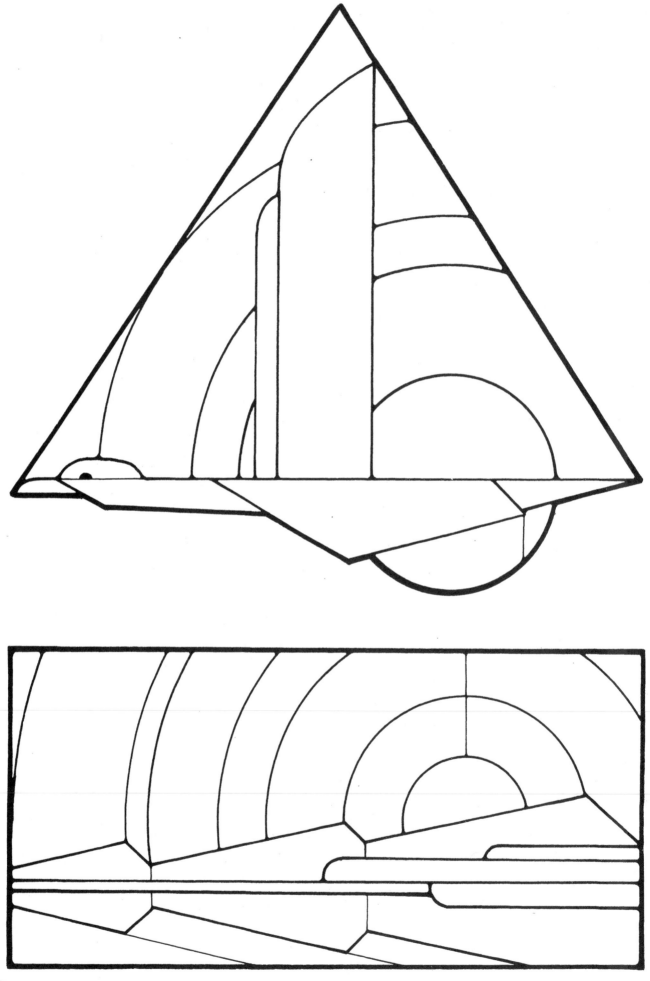

54

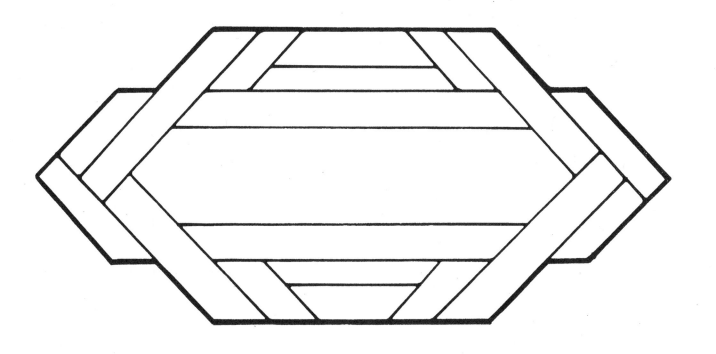

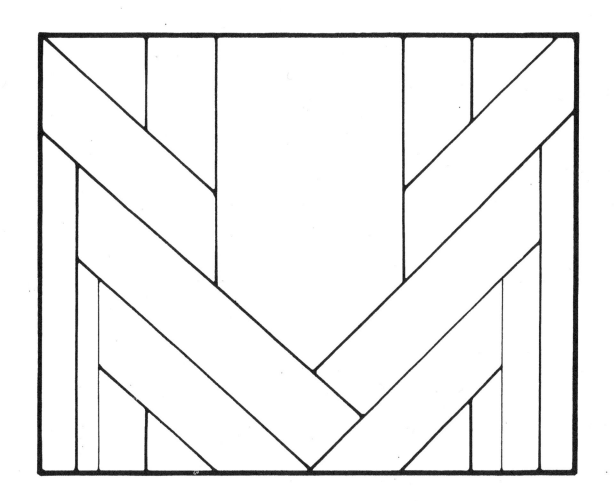

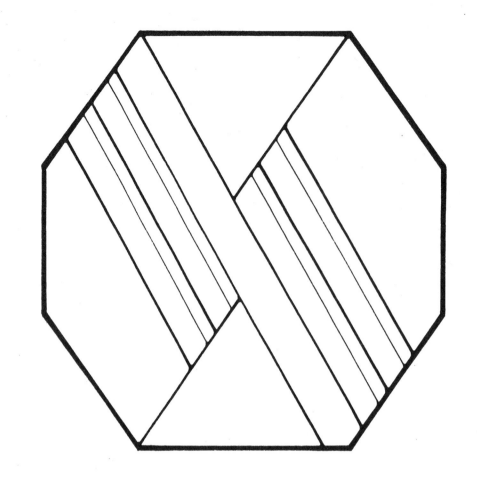

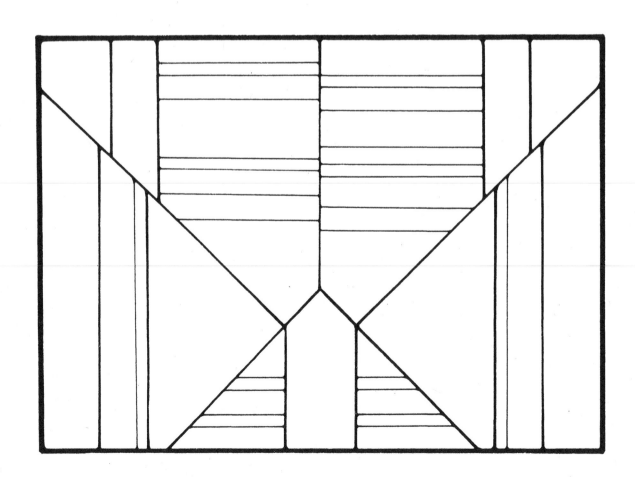

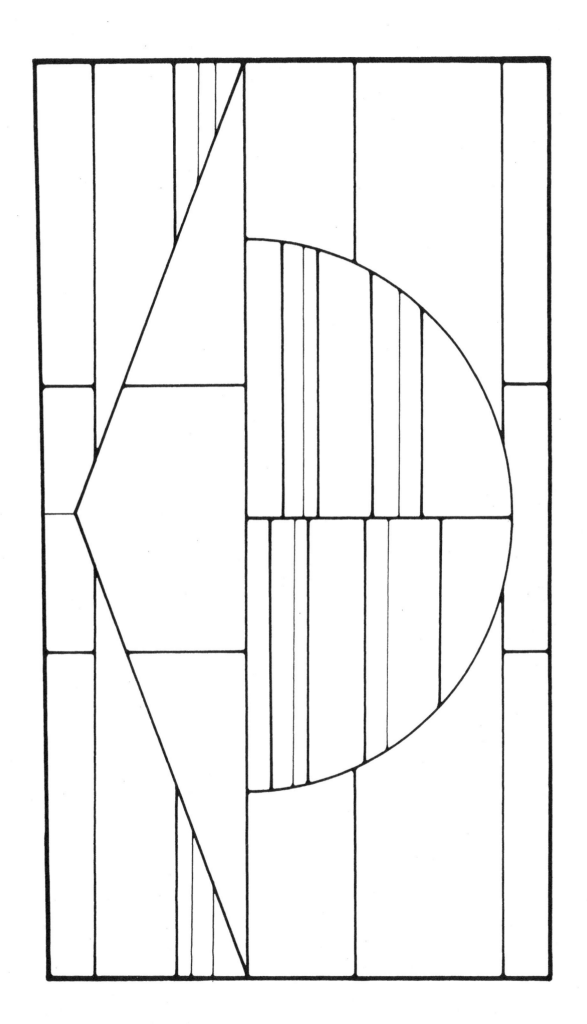

58

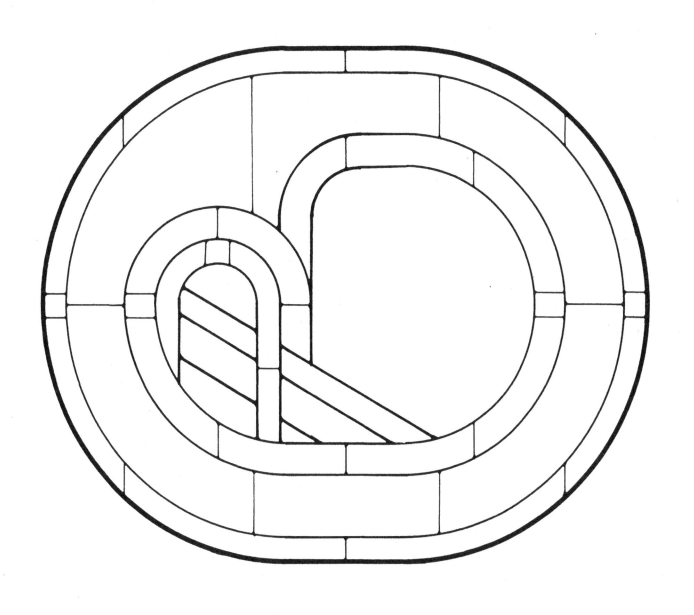

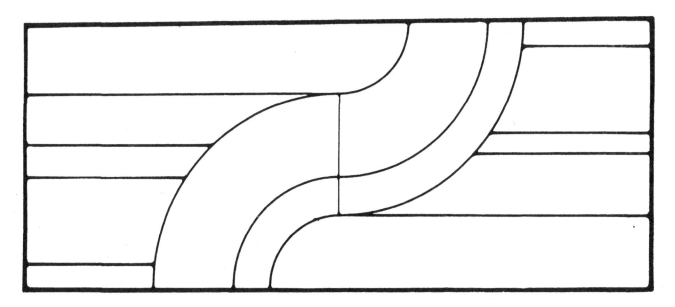

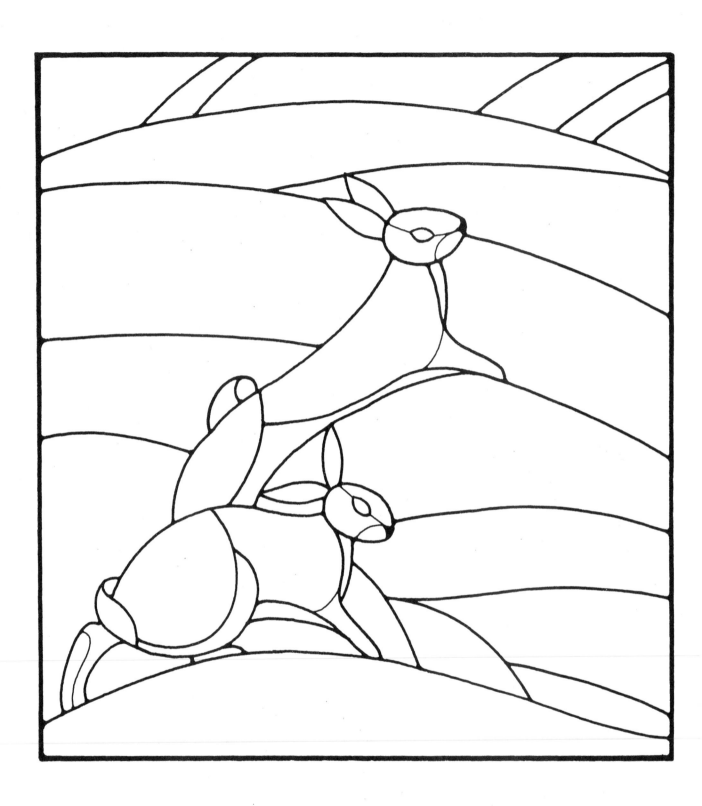

DOVER STAINED GLASS PATTERNS BOOKS

CONTEMPORARY DESIGNS FOR GLASS ETCHING, Sherri Boldt. (0-486-44534-8)

MANDALA STAINED GLASS PATTERN BOOK, Anna Croyle. (0-486-46605-1)

CONTEMPORARY DESIGNS STAINED GLASS PATTERN BOOK, Anna Croyle. (0-486-47176-4)

MODERN DESIGNS STAINED GLASS PATTERN BOOK, Anna Croyle. (0-486-44662-X)

DOORWAYS, WINDOWS & TRANSOMS STAINED GLASS PATTERN BOOK, Anna Croyle. (0-486-46235-8)

THE TECHNIQUE OF LEADED GLASS, Alastair Duncan. (0-486-42607-6)

CIRCULAR STAINED GLASS PATTERN BOOK: 60 FULL-PAGE DESIGNS, Connie Eaton. (0-486-24836-4)

SUNCATCHERS STAINED GLASS PATTERN BOOK: 120 DESIGNS, Connie Clough Eaton. (0-486-25470-4)

WILD ANIMALS STAINED GLASS PATTERN BOOK, Connie Clough Eaton. (0-486-29337-8)

TIFFANY WINDOWS STAINED GLASS PATTERN BOOK, Connie Clough Eaton. (0-486-29853-1)

EASY STAINED GLASS PATTERNS FOR TRADITIONAL DOORWAYS, Connie Clough Eaton. (0-486-42608-4)

ANGELS AND CHERUBS STAINED GLASS PATTERN BOOK, Connie Clough Eaton. (0-486-40170-7)

JAPANESE DESIGNS STAINED GLASS PATTERN BOOK, Connie Clough Eaton. (0-486-46115-7)

EASY VICTORIAN FLORALS STAINED GLASS PATTERN BOOK, Connie Clough Eaton. (0-486-44174-1)

NAUTICAL DESIGNS STAINED GLASS PATTERN BOOK, Connie Clough Eaton. (0-486-43298-X)

HOW TO DESIGN STAINED GLASS, Jennie French. (0-486-27753-4)

415 ORIGINAL DESIGNS FOR STAINED GLASS, Michael Gowen. (0-486-26175-1)

AUTHENTIC ART NOUVEAU STAINED GLASS DESIGNS IN FULL COLOR, M. J. Gradl. (0-486-24362-1)

NATURE'S SPLENDOR STAINED GLASS PATTERN BOOK, M. S. Hanson. (0-486-47029-6)

390 TRADITIONAL STAINED GLASS DESIGNS, Hywell G. Harris. (0-486-28964-8)

CREATING STAINED GLASS LAMPSHADES, James H. Hepburn. (0-486-41747-6)

FLOWERS AND FRUITS STAINED GLASS PATTERN BOOK, Carol Krez. (0-486-27942-1)

CELTIC STAINED GLASS PATTERN BOOK, Mallory Pearce. (0-486-40479-X)

BIRD DESIGNS STAINED GLASS PATTERN BOOK, Carolyn Relei. (0-486-25947-1)

MARINE ANIMALS STAINED GLASS PATTERN BOOK, Carolyn Relei. (0-486-27016-5)